THE LOWER BODY Golf Swing

by

Reeves Weedon P.G.A.

Jack Harris PhD

Grosvenor House
Publishing Limited

This book is published by
Grosvenor House Publishing Ltd
28-30 High Street, Guildford, Surrey, GU1 3EL.
www.grosvenorhousepublishing.co.uk

A CIP record for this book
is available from the British Library

ISBN 978-1-78148-903-1

THE MANUAL

Contents

Chapter 1

Introduction

a.   A simple instruction (flex the left knee down and up)

    1.   First golf lesson should be without a club (leg drill)

b.   Why it works.

    1.   Flow of energy coordinates

    2.   Power creates shape

    3.   The ground powers the swing

    4.   The legs create the rotation

    5.   Gravity must be able to work on the club

    6.   Pushing mass in the ground creates momentum

    7.   The hardest action in golf is to move the club; once it is going it will move itself: just hang on for the ride!

c.   Ground reaction forces

d.   Injury prevention

The lower body swing is easy to describe and quick to learn, but behind this simplicity lies basic physics and physiology, and years of study and experience. The swing can be learned in minutes, but as with most forms of human performance, it takes practice to maximise its full expression. And, also as with other forms of human performance, it is vitally important to get the few critical movements exactly right from the start.

When we see a golf swing, the eye is drawn to the dramatic movements of the golf club, therefore we naturally assume that the way to produce the swing is to heave the club around with the arms and shoulders. In reality, however, the power to move the club comes from the ground.

All instructions and descriptions in this manual are for right-handed golfers. If you are left-handed, please reverse them.

a.   A simple instruction

To produce a lower body swing, address a golf ball with a golf club, then flex the left knee and extend the right knee. Allow this lower body action to move the rest of the body, which should turn slightly to the right. The body weight will be to the left. Then reverse the knees: flex the right knee and extend the left knee quickly. This action will rotate the upper body to the left and provide an inertial impulse to accelerate the golf club towards the ball. The feel of the swing is more down and up than right and left. It is a swing, an athletic, dynamic movement.

1.   First golf lesson should be without a club (leg drill)

The best way to familiarise yourself with the feeling of the lower body swing is to do the exercise called the "leg drill." Stand holding hands with another golfer, both with knees and hips slightly flexed. Both now flex the left knee and extend the right knee, rotating the upper body to the right. Then reverse the knees, flexing the right knee and extending the left knee, rotating the upper body to the left. These actions will cause each person's arms to pull on their partner's arms. This should be the first lesson for a new lower body golfer.

b.   Why it works

The lower body swing works because pushing on the ground with the powerful leg and hip muscles causes rapid rotation of the upper body.

1.   Flow of energy coordinates

Scientists say, "The flow of energy through a system serves to organise that system."[1] The act of pushing on the ground provides the energy that flows

---

1   *Harold J. Morowitz, Energy Flow in Biology (New York/London: Academic Press, 1968).*

through the body and coordinates the correct sequence of movements to maximally accelerate the club towards the ball. The golfer is not required to master, or attend to, the myriad small movements that are required by other golf swings.

2.   Power creates shape

The most difficult action in golf is to move the club. This is why golfers often take a long time to get their swings started. Unlike other approaches, in the lower body swing the golfer doesn't move the club; they moves their legs. The club is moved passively. Once the club starts moving it will move itself; the golfer just hangs on.

3.   The ground powers the swing

In the lower body swing, the legs cause body rotation. Our measurements show that twice as much rotational momentum can be created in this way as in the conventional golf swing (see chapter 10).

4.   The legs create the rotation

In the lower body swing, pushing on the ground with the legs provides the necessary power.

5.   Gravity must be able to work on the club

The power that is provided by pushing the legs on the ground creates the shape of the swing, and ultimately the shape of the ball flight. Control of the shape of the ball flight is gained through power. In other words, the harder the ball is hit, the more control the golfer has over its trajectory.

6.   Pushing mass into the ground creates momentum

The more the golfer pushes into the ground, the more power and control are gained. As with athletic moves in other sports, the more the golfer pushes their mass into the ground, the more momentum is created.

7.   The hardest action in golf is to move the club; once it is going it will move itself: just hang on for the ride!

Because the lower body is doing the job of creating power, rotation and inertial impulse, the upper body is allowed to react to these forces. Importantly, because the upper body is not moving the club, gravity is allowed to act. This adds acceleration and shape to the swing, unlike conventional swings that require the club to be manipulated into the correct position.

c. Ground reaction forces

According to Newton's third law, for every action force there is an equal (in size) and opposite (in direction) reaction force. Forces always come in pairs, known as "action–reaction force pairs." Describing action–reaction force pairs is a simple matter of identifying the two interacting objects: in the lower body swing these are the pumping legs and the ground.

d. Injury prevention

The axis tilt, which is a sliding of the hips at the start of the downswing, starts the kinetic chain in the upper body (classic) golf swing. This bumping hip movement towards the target also shallows the shaft, regains loft on the clubface and creates a connection with the ground pre-impact. This motion, which is a must for the classic swing, puts too much torque on the spine and is a significant cause of lower back pain and injury in the golf swing.

The lower body swing has no axis tilt, therefore creates little or no torque on the spine and helps to prevent lower back injury.

An axis tilt in the golf swing is, in my opinion, like giving "arsenic for a bellyache!"

Chapter 2

How to teach yourself (or others) the lower body swing

a.   What is PPFPP?

1.   Unconditional positive regard

2.   Always first principles

3.   A few relentless principles

4.   Access new sensory modalities

5.   Iconoclasm

6.   New performance standards

7.   Either easy or impossible

8.   The subject will tell you when they get the hook

9.   Need to use alternative descriptors

b.   Useful images and phrases

c.   Pay attention to sound

d.   Look for high flight

e.   Transverse body pivot (front to back/back to front, feels down to up, and very left sided)

f.   Left arm under right shoulder

g.   The arms are dead/value the club's weight

Teaching the lower body swing, to yourself or to another golfer, is similar to coaching other forms of human performance, with perhaps one significant difference. That difference involves the necessity of convincing the student, particularly if that student has received previous golfing tuition, to trust that the ground will power the swing. No "help" from the arms, hands or shoulders is useful. Unlike the conventional swing, you do not need to try to turn your hips or shoulders: the force flowing through your body will look after these matters, if you allow them to.

Most golfing instruction teaches students about specific locations that the club and parts of the body are supposed to occupy at various stages of the swing. In the lower body swing, there are no positions. The flow of energy, if unimpeded, coordinates the correct phasing of movements. (For evidence, see chapter 10c.)

a.   What is PPFPP?

Having observed successful coaching sessions with golfers of varying levels of experience and ability, we have identified characteristics of interactions that are important to attend to. We call this attention "Psychological Priming for Physical Performance" (PPFPP). These are the principles of PPFPP:

1.   Unconditional positive regard

The coach must have unconditional positive regard for the student, especially if it is yourself. All comments and suggestions must be made in a positive light. Golf is played with a long lever arm, and the resultant leverage amplifies mistakes and can result in feelings of negativity. Positive regard and affirming comments build positive attitudes.

2.   Always first principles

Because learners are seldom familiar with using ground forces, the coach needs to focus relentlessly on the basic elements of the lower body swing. The energy from the ground will coordinate the body correctly. It is counter-productive to attend to the finer points such as grip, body positions or timing until later.

3.   A few relentless principles

The coach needs to be in the learner's head with phrases that will help the learner to concentrate on using the ground. This requires constant emphasis on

6

the coordinating principles of the lower body swing, particularly the transverse pivot.

4. Access new sensory modalities

It is helpful for learners to call to their attention sensory feedback they might otherwise ignore. Two examples are the sound of a well-struck shot and the height of a well-struck shot.

5. *Iconoclasm*

Most golfers bring with them an idea about how to achieve a golf swing. Learning the lower body swing usually requires forgetting this conventional – or even just wrong – information. For example, a beginner typically has erroneous ideas about the speed of the backswing and the downswing (the ground forces take care of these). The coach can assist the transition to the new swing by sustaining an iconoclastic attitude.

6. *New performance standards*

It is helpful for learners to call to their attention aspects of their performance they might otherwise ignore. Two examples are the distance of a shot and the shape of the trajectory (the draw). And the ball never starts to the left of its intended target.

7. *Either easy or impossible*

There is nothing difficult about the lower body swing. When the legs are moved correctly and the rest of the body is allowed to react, the ball will go up into the air and fly in a proper trajectory. The learner needs regular encouragement that it is easy and that they will be able to do it. The advantages of using the lower body swing are instantly visible. You just need to get out of the way of yourself and hang on to the Big Mo!

8. *The subject will tell you when they get the hook*

If the coach is paying attention, the student will unambiguously communicate to the coach which teaching approach was successful. The learner tells the coach when they "get the hook," but the telling will not be verbal. Coach and learner need to remain in constant communication, and the coach just has to tap into the learner's "lingo."

9. *Need to use alternative descriptors*

It usually takes several different approaches to communicate a change to a learner. The coach must try multiple metaphors and incorporate multiple images. Often the simplest formulations work best – for example, "big legs" is a better cue than "scientific studies show that flexing your left knee to 120 degrees is optimum."

b. Useful images and phrases

Certain phrases seem to be especially helpful in teaching the lower body swing. It is helpful if these phrases are repeated quietly while the golfer is beginning the swing. The effect is to replace the golfer's unhelpful swing thoughts with more productive ones. Here are some examples:

- "Come out of golf." As long as the golfer is attempting to match their movements to an idealised set of movements, they will interfere with the flow of energy. This phrase encourages the golfer to try something new.

- "Let it go." This is another way of encouraging the golfer to allow the ground forces to move their body. This applies as much on the backswing as on the downswing.

- "The arms are dead." This means not engaging the muscles of the arms and shoulders.

- "Heavy arms." This also means not engaging arm and shoulder muscles.

- "What's heavy going up is light coming down." Most poor golfers reverse this, snatching the club upwards and fighting to move it down fast.

- "Value the weight of the club." This is an alternative sensory modality to call to the learner's attention. Many poor golfers are oblivious to the weight of the club, particularly with longer clubs.

- "Let gravity work on the club." If the arms are passive and if the club is heavy going up, then gravity will act on the club, adding acceleration and allowing the club to fall into the position that creates "lag," the timing that maximises power.

- "Poor players are in a hurry to get down; good players want never to get there." Time at the top allows gravity to work on the club and power from the legs to coordinate the body.

- "Go down and up." The lower body swing feels very vertical. It is necessary to come up in order to clear space for the club.

- "When the shaft and the neck meet, the swing is complete." Learners need to embrace the momentum created by the ground.

- "The ball is your target." Learners frequently worry about a distant target such as a green and ignore the ball. All golfers have this problem when they move from practice tee to the course.

c. Pay attention to sound

The lower body swing delivers the club to the ball with maximum force and square alignment. One result is the loud "pop" of a properly struck ball. A loud noise is an indicator of a correctly executed swing.

d. Look for high flight

The lower body swing maintains loft on the club through the swing. Consequently the ball flight will be high. High flight adds distance and control, and is an indicator of a correctly executed swing.

e. Transverse body pivot

The core of the lower body swing is the transverse pivot. If the legs are moved in the correct way and the upper body remains passive, then the weight will move from front to back and then from back to front. The feeling is of going down and up and is very left sided.

f. Left arm under right shoulder

In the lower body swing there is no axis tilt. (This refers to a feature of the conventional swing that requires the body to kink sidewards towards the right hand to avoid the club hitting the right shoulder.) Because the left arm is below the right shoulder, gravity is allowed to work on the club so that it can fall without hitting the right shoulder. An aligned axis helps to prevent back injuries and maintains loft on the clubface.

g.   The arms are dead/value the club's weight

When the legs drive the transverse pivot and the upper body remains passive, the angle assumed by the body at address will cause the club to rise. The arms do not raise the club. At the top of the backswing the left arm is across the chest, and it does not rise above the right shoulder. The club is necessarily in a position of "heavy lag." This means it is the final element in a chain of moving parts. This allows gravity to act on the club and increase power.

Chapter 3

How the lower body swing creates the seven phases

a. Phase, not position.

b. Allow the ground to cause them to happen.

a. Phase, not position

In my book, *The Phase Seven Golf Swing*,[2] I set out the basics of the lower body swing. As the title suggests, the book focuses on the phases through which the club passes during the swing. In physics, "phase" is a comparison of the relative position of two things. In the book I describe the relative positions of the clubhead to the body.

We have sought the clues that would correctly put golfers through the phases. Over time we have come to see that by concentrating on the production of ground force couples through proper use of the large leg and hip muscles, the phases happen by themselves.

b. Allow the ground to cause them to happen

Please understand that "phases" are not "positions." Each phase is a section of a sequence of continuous movement. It will not work to "put" the club in certain places because the swing is dynamic, like a line of falling dominoes: all that is needed is a starting impulse. The seven phases are descriptive, not proscriptive. This means that the golfer does not seek to learn, practise or master these phases

---

2 *Reeves Weedon, The Phase Seven Golf Swing, Pennington: Mountain Lion, 2012.*

(as do golfers practising the kinetic sequence in the conventional swing), but rather to allow the ground reaction force to move their body and club.

The physics underlying the lower body swing is described in chapter 10, but it is worth stating here that the lower body swing makes three physics-based improvements on the conventional swing. First, it maximises the conservation of angular momentum by not dissipating it in lateral moves. Secondly, it keeps the moment of inertia low (so the ground force can generate maximum clubhead speed) by keeping the body collected together and the club close. Thirdly, the lower body swing creates an inertial impulse that reroutes the club at the top of the backswing so that no energy-wasting "transition" move is required.

The power produced by the legs will naturally take the player through the phases, as long as there is no tampering with body and club movements. The power creates the shape of body and club movements, and it creates the shape of the ball flight. Nonetheless, understanding the phases is useful for coaches and learners to understand how the ground moves the body and the club during the lower body swing, and to have a language to discuss how to improve the swing.

The following chapter contains pictorial descriptions of the phase seven swing (lower body swing).

Chapter 4

Checkpoints

a. Left knee over left foot

b. Left arm over chest

c. Right leg straight

d. Weight left

e. Both legs jump

f. Ball is the target

g. Ball position

h. No axis tilt

i. Left knee/right knee/hip and shoulder

j. Left arm under right shoulder

k. Resist the throw-out/access gravity

l. Loft on the clubface

m. Arms have the same characteristics as the body

a.   Left knee over left foot

b.   Left arm over chest

c.   Right leg straight

d.   Weight left

e. Both legs jump

f. Ball is the target

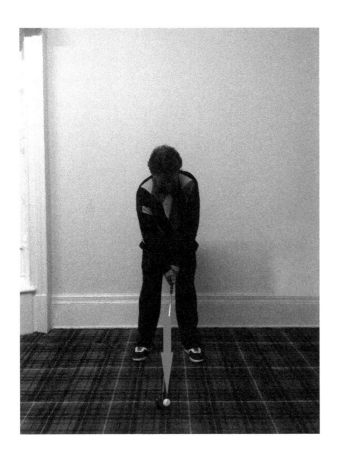

g.   Ball position

h.   No axis tilt

i. Left knee/right knee/hip and shoulder

j. Left arm under right shoulder

k. Resist the throw-out/ access gravity

l. Loft on the clubface

m. Arms have the same characteristics as the body

Chapter 5

Faults, fixes and drills

a.   Arms lift

b.   Not valuing weight of club

c.   Missing the ball

d/e. Topping the ball/Thinning the ball

f.   Slicing

g.   Hooking

h.   Needing more distance

The lower body swing makes maximum use of the laws of physics and facts of human physiology. It is easy to learn and straightforward to teach. However, as with other forms of human performance, attaining skill takes practice. And, as with other forms of human performance, getting started correctly with the (few) basics can help to prevent many later problems. The trained eye of a coach or professional can also help to prevent problems by monitoring the learner's thoughts and movements as their skills develop.

   Golf is a demanding game, and all players need to reconnect with the basics in order to be successful, so regular lessons are to be recommended. In golf there are many common pitfalls. Returning to the basics – the transverse pivot, club no higher than right shoulder, and big legs – fixes most problems. With reference to these few basics, here are some examples of particular swing flaws and ways to fix them:

a. Arms lift

Cause: arms swinging away from the body as the first move. Also, the arms moving away from the body centre.

Fix: flexing left knee/extending right knee starts the golf swing (and the process of pushing into the ground). The arms then move in the direction of the body.

b. Not valuing weight of club

Causes: the arms initiate backswing lift which creates lack of momentum. Alternatively, the arms accelerate towards the ball on the downswing, which decreases loft and misses the centre of the strike.

Fix: using the ground. The legs power the backswing, the arms do nothing and are moved by body motion. Also, the inertial impulse of the legs pushing on the ground throws the club into the ball, without additional arm action. It is important to retain soft, free wrists.

c. Missing the ball

Causes: forgetting that the ball is your target; having only peripheral (or no) vision of the ball; acceleration or deceleration by the arms; weight shift not caused by the transverse pivot; shortening the lever arm by bending the elbows.

Fixes: first teach the learner to swing and miss the ball intentionally; use the drills that teach that what is heavy going up is light going down; help the golfer to feel gravity working on the downswing; make sure the ball is in the golfer's central vision. Repetition!

d/e. Topping the ball/Thinning the ball

Causes: lever shortening caused by shoulder tilting not related to the transverse pivot; tight wrists; acceleration or deceleration not caused by the transverse pivot; having only peripheral (or no) vision of the ball.

Fixes: the transverse pivot; soft, free wrists; drills that teach that what is heavy going up is light coming down; left arm remains below right shoulder; allowing gravity to work on the club.

f. Slicing

Causes: arms lifting; weight shifting laterally; acceleration from the top unrelated to legs pushing on the ground ("casting"); tightness in grip, wrists, hands or shoulders; set-up to ball wrong (ball too far forward; body aimed incorrectly); grip too weak.

Fixes: the transverse pivot; accessing gravity; using the ground; relaxed upper body; ensuring that arm movement has same characteristics as body movement; left arm under right shoulder; ball position near middle of stance.

g.   Hooking

Causes: set-up issues, such as standing too far away from the ball; shoulders and hips aimed to the right; grip too strong; weight shift too right-sided in the downswing; body slowing at impact while club maintains maximum speed; grip too loose.

Fixes: transverse pivot; using the ground; ensuring that arm movement has same characteristics as body movement; left arm under right shoulder; accessing gravity.

h.   Needing more distance

Causes: not accessing the ground; blocking the acceleration caused by the transverse pivot; moving everything too slowly.

Fix: allowing the legs to turn the lower body on the backswing and the inertial impulse produced by the legs to power the downswing.

Chapter 6

Teaching

a. Challenges

    1. Attitude

    2. Talent

    3. Focus

b. Groups

c. It doesn't look normal!

a.   Challenges

When it comes to teaching the lower body swing, many players think they know enough about the golf swing in general but may not know how to learn it. They get caught up in truths that have always let them down and become confused with the simplicity of our coaching methods. My answer to this problem is always, "Get out of golf!"

Once you stop thinking "golf swing," the lower body swing is very simple and achievable. Golf is an illogical game played by logical people. I say constantly to my students, "If it makes sense, don't believe it!"

The way people learn is based on the information given, and everyone does it a little differently. Some just want to think about their motion; others want to feel it, see it or just do it!

So the coach must always listen to what the learner is saying, as they always say what they want to be taught. The lower body swing coach uses their ears more than their mouth.

The moral of our learning is the acronym KISS – Keep It Simple, Stupid. If you come out of golf you will experience a unique kinaesthetic feel that will stripe it every time!

1. Attitude

Although it is widely known that there are four types of learners – people who do, people who feel, people who see and people who think – in my experience there are only two: people who want, and people who don't want. Those who want, I call "students of the game" – they want to achieve their best golf. The don't wants I call "Rodeo ponies" – you might as well enjoy the ride before they buck you off!

The students are people with little or no opinion of how the swing works. They will follow your instructions verbatim and be patient with their improvement. Other students in this category are those who have tried every method to no avail and are almost ready to give up, but don't want to. I find such people to be good learners because their past opinions have disappeared as a result of multiple failures. They cling to the rapid success of lower body swing and improve like never before.

Rodeo ponies spend more time telling you about what they are doing than listening to what they need to do. They are so caught up in technique that they are oblivious to the instruction, "Come out of golf!" They are, as we have said, logical people playing an illogical game. Rodeo ponies will book sessions with the lower body swing coach through recommendations from their friends who are playing unbelievably well. However, these students are not prepared to make changes like their friends have. The old adage comes to mind: "If you change nothing, nothing changes." And the Rodeos refuse to change because they cannot understand the simplicity of coming out of golf in order to change their future. It reminds me of Einstein's definition of madness: "Man repeating the same thing, expecting change."

Having the right attitude is crucial to being a good learner.

2. Talent

Another word for talent, in my opinion, is "recovery." People who recover their swing the most are those their peers refer to as talented. Talent is not as important to learning the lower body swing as attitude and focus. Talent will increase the purpose if the pupil is focused on the change in hand and has a good attitude. As a rule of thumb, if people are skilled at a particular game, they tend to play it more. Without practice and repetition they will not achieve the heights of success of which they are capable. A good attitude and focus are paramount to learning the lower body swing. Talent is an optional extra.

3. Focus

When people choose golf as their main sporting activity, most assume they will be able to play a decent game. But often this is not the case, and in many cases year after year they do not attain the standard they wish for. Millions of golfers have devoted enough time and effort to their game to have attained a high standard if they had focused more on the correct things.

It pays to focus more on the ground that powers the swing. The legs that flex and extend against the ground push power into the body to coordinate the internal flow of energy. In the lower body swing, we believe that if you focus on the physical power created by the body's relationship with the ground, it will recruit the correct muscles to enable the golfer to hit the ball like an elite player. Focus is important. Focus on what is correct to science, not to the latest teaching fad.

b. Groups

It is simple to teach the lower body swing to groups. Through ground-force dynamics, we believe that all students will be able to improve ball flight and increase distance. Group tuition is greatly assisted by use of two lower body drills.

The first of these is called the beginner's drill (leg drill). This introduces all golfers to the power of the ground on which we stand. Pushing in and against the ground creates power that the ordinary golfer will rarely have experienced. Here's how it goes.

Without a club, assume the address position, with arms hanging freely in front of the body. Then start pumping the legs, flexing the left leg at the knee and straightening the right leg simultaneously in order to rotate the core. This leg motion masters the rotary swing around a fixed axis (the spine). Be sure to keep your head steady. Continue to flex and extend the legs alternately, pushing into and off the ground until you build a good rhythm. Practise this drill for about five minutes every day, and you will develop a strong pivot to power the swing.

The other drill is called the flamingo drill. The name gives the task away. Stand on your left leg and raise your right leg in the air. Take a club in your right hand and pivot clockwise until your right shoulder and hip are behind you. Pause momentarily and then pivot anticlockwise to initiate striking a ball. Keep doing this until you feel your muscles ache. This drill will give you the feeling of a centred pivot, and will provide depth in the swing that will enhance its power. As with the beginner's drill, five minutes a day will create a muscle memory which will power the swing like never before.

It is simple to teach the lower body swing to large groups of golfers, and they will make rapid improvement. Using golf drills is a must in group coaching.

c. It doesn't look normal!

Dick Fosbury used the "Fosbury Flop," a then unorthodox head-first back-to-the-bar method of high jumping, at the Mexico City Olympic Games in 1968. He cleared seven feet, four and a half inches to secure a gold medal and a world record. His method was later identified scientifically to be superior because it keeps the centre of the body mass below the bar. Before Fosbury, every high jumper went over the bar on their belly; after Fosbury, every high jumper did it his way.

A similar paradigm shift is now happening in the more popular game of golf because the lower body swing is pure to scientific truths:

- The ground powers the swing.

- The moment of inertia is small.

- The mass to hit the ball is greater.

- Gravity can access the club.

- It abides by the law of Conservation of Angular Momentum and Newton's three laws of force and motion.

So we took a big pot, put in all the above scientific components and mixed it up, not knowing quite what it would look like. It came out looking like the lower body golf swing, and it is pure and correct.

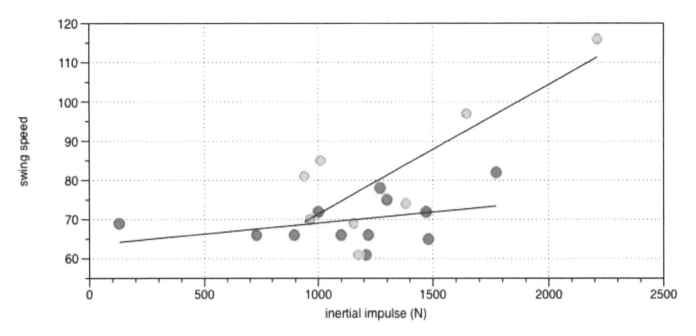

This graph charts the swing speeds of scratch golfers (green) and handicap golfers (red) against the total inertial impulse (force exerted on ground from top of backswing till impact). The two linear regression lines show that for the same impulse a scratch golfer has higher swing speed. For example, the linear regression lines show that at 1500 N inertial impulse, a handicap golfer would be expected to have 72mph swing speed, and a scratch golfer 88mph swing speed. This is an improvement of approximately 20% (or over 30 yards for a seven-iron hit 160 yards).

This difference in converting inertial impulse into swing speed is caused by faulty mechanics in the handicap golfer – typically, involving extraneous upper body motions. So what the coach is doing in the lower body swing is getting the student to climb on to the steeper regression line!

Chapter 7

Special situations

a.   Uphill lie

b.   Downhill lie

c   Ball above your feet

d.   Ball below your feet

e.   High flight shot

f.   Lower flight shot

g.   Draw the ball

h.   Fade the ball

i.   Chipping (a short shot)

j.   Pitching (longer and higher than a chip)

These are commonly known as awkward lies or speciality shots. Adjustments are usually made before the shot takes place so that the swing's environment is as normal. These shots are important to all golfers as they are the epoxy (glue) to every golfer's round.

a.   Uphill lie

- Weight on the lower foot, so the body is perpendicular to the slope.
- Position the ball closer to the higher foot.

- Aim the blade and body to the right of your intended target.

- Swing as normal and the ball should fly right to left.

- For the uphill lie, always select more club as the height you will attain off the slope will mean loss of distance.

b. Downhill lie

- Weight on the lower foot, so the body is perpendicular to the slope.

- Position the ball nearer to the higher foot.

- Aim the blade and body to the left of the intended target.

- Swing as normal and the ball should fly left to right.

- Select less club as the slope will deloft the club and the ball will fly lower and further.

c. Ball above your feet

- Stand closer to the ball and grip the club slightly lower than usual.

- Weight should be evenly balanced.

- Ball should be positioned in the middle of the stance.

- Aim blade and body to the right of the target.

- Swing as normal and you should hit a right-to-left shot.

d. Ball below your feet

- Lower your centre of gravity at address by flexing your knees more. Retain this knee flex throughout the swing.

- Weight should be evenly balanced.

- Ball should be positioned left of centre.

- Aim blade and body to the left of the target.

- Swing as normal, retaining more flex in the knees, and you should hit a left-to-right-shot.

e. High flight shot

This shot is simple to achieve with the lower body swing:

- Grip higher than usual on the club.

- Use more wrists.

- Grip pressure will be less (softer).

- Use the ground more. By doing this you will gain more length, along with a centred strike.

f. Lower flight shot

To produce a lower flight shot the principle is also simple. The task is to turn your two-lever system swing into one. It will resemble a long chip shot swing and will keep the ball flight down. To create a one-lever, tighten the wrist joint to make the arm and club work as a single unit from shoulder to clubhead.

- Grip the club lower to shorten the leverage.

- Tighten grip pressure and freeze the wrists.

- Use the ground less. By doing this you will also lose distance.

g. Draw the ball

The draw shot is produced before the shot is made, in the address. Simply move the ball back in your stance towards your back foot (for the right-handed player) and towards the toe on the clubface. Then swing as normal and enjoy the fruit of a soft draw.

h. Fade the ball

As with the draw, the fade is produced pre-shot. The ball is moved towards the player's front foot and towards the heel of the club. When swinging normally, a soft fade will appear.

Note: Do not accelerate at the ball with this shot. A better result will be attained by slowing down at impact.

i. Chipping (a short shot)

A chip shot is a one-lever movement. As in the low shot, simply freeze the wrist joint to make the arms and club move as one from shoulder to clubhead.

- Weight as normal. You may favour the front foot.
- Feet should be closer together than for a normal shot.
- Ball position middle/back.
- Aim as normal.
- Stand closer to the ball.
- Swing. As in a full swing, the legs power the chip shot by flexing and extending against the ground, although not as much, as less power is needed. The club doesn't go above the hips.

j. Pitching (longer and higher than a chip)

This uses the same technique as the chip shot but with the two-lever model. Defrost the wrists. The club swings higher than the hips, but not as high as in a full shot.

Chapter 8

Tailored teaching

a.   Common challenges

   1.   Rigidity

   2.   Floppy looseness

   3.   Physical limitations

   4.   Lack of athletic experience

b.   Beginners

c.   Women

d.   Children

e.   The elderly

f.   Those with disabilities

The future of golf depends on including all people. Golf offers terrific exercise, opportunities for social interaction, competition and kinaesthetic pleasure. But there are significant barriers to entry for much of the population. The biggest barrier may be the perception that golf is difficult to learn and that it takes a long time to become competent.

The lower body swing offers the possibility of reducing the barriers to competency for populations who do not currently play golf. Experience shows that in the first lesson, a student using the lower body swing – be they an adult, a child or a senior – can strike the ball solidly and get it up in the air. After a few lessons, and some practice, a student can become competent enough to play most courses.

At present, golf is dominated by men of working age, women of working age (who often face serious discrimination with regard to access to facilities and instruction) and retired people who learned to play when they were younger. There are golf programmes for juniors, but these are usually filled with the children of adult golfers. In this section we will consider how to use the lower body swing to coach populations that are currently under-represented.

There are general principles that apply to working with all these populations, even though, of course, specific details need to be devised for each person. These are general principles that apply to teaching any new activity, particularly if the activity requires observed performance.

First, the student needs to feel that they are successful and don't appear foolish. Secondly, the student needs a conceptual framework and the physical experience of the feel of the ground force. All of the coaching techniques discussed in chapter 1 of this manual need to be ramped up, and the most important of these is a consistent positive attitude and message from the coach.

a. Common challenges

Here are some of the common challenges and fixes when tailoring coaching to the learner:

1. Rigidity

Causes: trying too hard; fear of failure; physical limitations; achievement orientation.

Fixes: lightness; celebrating successes; simple movements.

2. Floppy looseness

Causes: lack of athletic experience; no feeling for source of power.

Fixes: feeling the ground forces.

3. Physical limitations

Causes: many, including muscular/skeletal disorders, arthritis, eyesight, trauma.

Fixes: honest discussion; then accommodation to the movements of the transverse pivot.

4. *Lack of athletic experience*

Causes: lack of opportunity; fear.

Fixes: patience; focus on fundamentals.

b. Beginners

To most beginning adults the golf swing is non-intuitive. The golf grip seems contrived. Turning your back to the target sounds like lunacy. As it is usually presented, the golf swing consists of thousands of moving parts that all require perfect timing. And it seems obvious that the only way to hit the ball far is to swing the club as fast as possible.

The lower body swing massively reduces the chaos. Details that are usually focused on in conventional lessons – such as grip, stance, wrist cock, straight left arm – can all be ignored until much later. Once the student feels the club being moved by the inertial impulse generated through simple leg motions, they will be on the path to continued improvement.

The student is likely to expect either to perform like a professional or to fail utterly (perhaps as they have done in the past), so the coach needs to celebrate more prosaic milestones, such as the first ball struck, the first ball in the air, the first draw shape. The coach needs to counsel patience and repetition, and to be constantly feeding the student useful swing thoughts.

c. Women

Women beginners take well to the lower body swing since, statistically, most of their strength is in the lower body and they have less experience than men at flailing at things with their arms. It remains critically important, however, that women feel the power that flows through their body from the ground forces and that they allow that power to shape and time their swings.

Women who have played some golf will face the same challenges as men do in letting go of ingrained swing thoughts and habits.

d. Children

Children need short, intense lessons, and lots of praise. Young children often have a vast range of movement and can be slow to channel movements to the essential. It takes real care to enable a small child to feel the flow of power from the ground force couples. Playing with bigger, foam balls should be explored.

Older children benefit from repetition, which can be elicited with games and challenges.

e. The elderly

When teaching the lower body swing to a senior, it is important to recognise that as the body ages, there is a gradual loss of strength along with a reduction in flexibility as deterioration of the muscular system reduces movement and speed. This will lead to the senior losing distance through the green. The transverse body pivoting against the ground through flexion and extension of the legs will regain the power in the swing that is lost as a result of ageing. The lower body swing is a must for all seniors who want to prolong their golfing career.

f. Those with disabilities

When we speak of handicaps in golf, we immediately identify a player's ability through a number (a 24 or 6 handicap, for example). But there are golfers who play with other handicaps: those who are disabled. Whether the game is played by someone with a physical or a mental disability, golf should be a game that all can enjoy and reach a proficient standard.

The coach is probably more important in determining the success of the lesson programme for a learner with a disability than for any other learner. While all individuals, when being coached, must provide their own motivation, enthusiasm and patience, the coach can be supportive and sustain additional motivation and encouragement with those who face additional challenges.

The lower body swing coach, with their special teaching tools, can enable the learner to add power to the swing through wrists, legs or body during the teaching sessions.

Chapter 9

Case studies

a. Beginner

b. High handicapper

c. Low handicapper

d. Scratch player

e. Player with disabilities

a. Beginner

When working with a person who has never made a golf swing before, the first step would be an introduction to the ground we stand on. The ground provides the power to the swing, so the first thing to teach would be the beginner's leg drill.

This drill calls for an emphasis on a pumping action, or flexing of the left leg at the knee and rotation at the core. This is how the motion is produced: flex the left knee out towards the target line on which the ball sits. Extend the right leg as much as possible. Next, turn the right shoulder in or around to the back, away from the target line in a clockwise motion. When the right shoulder is turned approximately 90 degrees, the leg action can keep moving to push as much body mass into the ground as possible. Your core legs and shoulders have created muscular tension. Your feet are pressing into the ground, creating more force that will be released when the legs start pushing against the ground.

This alternate flexion and extension of the legs must be taken to the practice tee after the coaching session has finished. This drill will give the golf shot effortless power.

Once we have repeated this drill several times, the learner is given a golf club and asked on the backswing, after holding the club and addressing the ball, to flex the left leg and extend the right leg. Then on the downswing, to extend the left leg and flex the right leg. This takes place while allowing gravity to access the club and making a motion with the club at the ball.

The simplicity of this movement always gives flight to the ball in a beginner's first golf lesson. The layperson can understand and coordinate their weight, pressing down into the ground on the backswing as the club goes up. And as the weight is pushed up from the ground on the downswing, the club is thrown down at the ball.

The beginner's drill is essential for all learner golfers.

b. High handicapper

As with the beginner, we would hypothesise that this player's connection with the ground is poor as a result of their handicap. If this is the case, we would ask them to learn and practise the beginner's leg drill. Once the learner has mastered this drill sufficiently, loft on the clubface is a must to fit with the new weight shift.

Loft on the clubface is crucial for all lower body swing players. We are not interested in a square, open or closed clubface at the top of the backswing; rather we are interested in loft on the clubface so that we can access gravity and hit the ball with maximum mass. Loft is attained with the grooves of the club pointing towards the sky. This skyward orientation will guarantee maximum height on the ball flight, that is trajectory equal to the respective degrees of loft on the particular club.

This clubface position brings the whole club in line with the body so it can access gravity and master a pivot that is as close as possible to a 100-percent rotation. This will create a small moment of inertia and provide the necessary mass to hit the ball.

These two changes to this player's swing will catapult their handicap to a lower number, if learnt well.

c. Low handicapper

A golfer with a low handicap needs to learn three main skills to propel them to golf that they never dreamed of. Along with the injury reduction aspect of the lower body swing, the following three skills are essential to quality ball striking.

The first would be to introduce the player to the ground, to drive the swing. As we have said before, the flexing and extending of the legs at the knees creates the rotation that keeps the body over the ball and prevents drifting. During the pivot, the feet push down hard on the turf, allowing the hips to swivel or turn around the fixed access of the spine. The ground pushes upwards, friction keeping the feet in place, the head over the ball and the torso centred between the feet. The result of these powerful opposing forces is the formation of a rock-solid platform to power the swing's pivot.

The core of the body, which controls this pivot, harnesses the power of the body's mass as it turns around the spine. The magnitude of this power is raised by increasing the downward pressure of the feet and gravity because, as Newton's third law predicts, it produces an equal force that pushes upwards. The significant force needed to rotate the body's core is greatly assisted by this powered base. The rotation of the body mass takes place on the body's transverse plane, which dissects the body along a plane that is perpendicular to the angle of the spine. This kinetic sequence requires dynamic balance to prevent any lateral leakage. To put this into layman's language, the down-and-up weight shift against the ground, which is a vertical force, creates pure rotation! Telling the learner to rotate will create lateral movement. This vertical force will create massive power.

The second skill is to put loft on the clubface. As for the player with a higher handicap, the grooves of the clubface point skywards. This skyward clubface position will guarantee maximum height of the ball flight and prodigious distance along with the ground forces applied.

Once the elite player has tapped into the vertical forces and loft has been accessed, the last skill to be learnt is to make the golfer's moment of inertia small. This will be done by keeping the left arm under the right shoulder, enabling the sweet spot of the clubface to be closer to the body's centre of rotation, the spine. The moment of inertia is a measure of the opposition that a body (the clubhead) exhibits to its speed around an axis, which may or may not be fixed. The left arm under the right shoulder makes the distance from the body's rotational centre shorter, which allows the body to move faster and to deliver all the energy created and stored into the ball. This in turn will fly the ball to the target.

So to recap: three essential skills must be learnt by a player with a low handicap to take them into the professional ranks:

- Down-and-up weight shift

- Loft on the clubface

- Left arm under the right shoulder.

d. Scratch player

The scratch player, along with the player with a low handicap, must learn the three skills:

- Down-and-up weight shift

- Loft on the clubface
- Left arm under the right shoulder.

To reach a professional standard, these skills must be mastered. In addition, the player must be taught grip pressures, swing tempos and an understanding of how gravity can add power to the swing.

e. Player with disabilities

It is important for the professional coach to gain some basic knowledge about the learner's disability during the introduction to the lesson. Enquire about any physical, psychological or medical limitations. It is also important to find out the learner's motive for taking instruction. If they have been sent by a doctor or therapist, there might not be much fun in the lesson as the pupil might see it as rehabilitation rather than sport. If this is the case, finding a physically challenged partner to learn with might be helpful. While all individuals must provide their own motivation, an enthusiastic, supportive, patient and persevering coach means so much to a disadvantaged player who may be struggling to muster enthusiasm.

When teaching the lower body swing to a disabled learner, progress will be made by use of tools of learning which hopefully will encourage the player to enjoy golf again, so that they will look forward once more to playing a round. With all disabilities, improvement in the player's ball flight will push them to a credible level of competence. We are also confident that a good standard of rehabilitation will take place during the teaching sessions.

Chapter 10

More advanced analysis

a. Relevant physics

  1. Newton's three laws

  2. Pushing mass into the ground creates momentum

b. Basics of the lower body swing

  1. Loft

  2. No axis tilt

  3. Where is "behind the ball?"

  4. Resist the throw-out

  5. Small moment of inertia creates bigger mass to hit with

c. Research

  1. Purpose

  2. Methods

  3. Results

  4. Conclusions

d. Unknowns that need to be investigated

a. Relevant physics

1. Newton's three laws

For a long time now, golf coaches have had the task of teaching swings to their students. Like all fashions, new methods spring up every year. Like clockwork, the old methods vanish and new ones appear. This is an ongoing problem for the jobbing golf coach. There are so many different ideas, and the continual changes create problems for credible information.

But let's get out of teaching fads and delve into the real substance – physics! This is obviously the tool that drives every machine – even the golf swing. Let us introduce every golfer to the genius of Sir Isaac Newton, the greatest golf coach of them all!

Newton was a physicist whose laws of classical mechanics first explained motion in the seventeenth century. We believe his three laws of force and motion should be in the toolbox of every sports coach! If there is no understanding of these laws, we believe golf, and sport in general, cannot be taught correctly.

The power creates the shape of the swing. Newton's three laws – (1) inertia; (2) acceleration; and (3) action–reaction – provide coaches with a solid understanding of mechanical cause and effect in the swing. Force creates motion.

2. *Pushing mass into the ground creates momentum*

As discussed earlier, Newton's third law says that for every action force there is a reaction force, equal in size and opposite in direction. Forces always come in pairs, known as action–reaction pairs. Describing action–reaction force pairs is a simple matter of identifying the *two* interacting objects and making two statements describing who is *pushing* on whom and in what *direction*. The flexing and extending of the legs at the knees creates the rotation of the body.

This pushing against the ground and pushing up feels as if you are going down and up. This is called 'vertical force'. This vertical force creates pure rotation above the knees. It's a paradox: the more you push down into the ground, the more you can push up. Pushing your mass into the ground through your legs creates the Big Mo!

b. Basics of the lower body swing

1. *Loft*

At the top of the backswing, the grooves of the clubface will point towards the sky. Golfers should not care whether their clubface is square, closed or open. They should just care that there is loft on the face. This will allow gravity to access the club and drop it into the impact zone. This clubface position will guarantee maximum height on your ball flight, that is a trajectory equal to the respective degrees of loft of the particular iron or wood. With this clubface position, it is difficult to hook the ball now there is no axis tilt in the swing.

2. *No axis tilt*

In the lower body swing we have taken out the axis tilt, which is vital to the classic upper body swing. This sliding of the hips at the start of the downswing sets off the kinetic chain and begins the shallowing of the shaft and regaining loft on the clubface. It also enables the upper body swinger to make contact with the ground pre-impact, to power the body. In theory, the weight of the upper body swinger goes up on the backswing, down on the downswing and then pushes up again pre-impact.

The lower body swinger has no axis tilt. The body weight goes down into the ground when the club goes up and around. This is where the kinetic chain starts. Then, when the club comes down, the weight is pushed up off the ground. Gravity can now access the club and drop it into the impact zone. The lower body player has no reason to retain loft on the face as it never left it, and has no need for the club to be shallowed out.

The axis tilt puts too much torque on the spine and is a great cause of injury in golf. As we mentioned before, we believe that putting the axis tilt in a golf swing is like giving arsenic for a bellyache!

3. *Where is "behind the ball?"*

Behind the ball is behind your head. When the arms have the same characteristics as the transverse body pivot, the right side of your body, hips and shoulders go behind you. The coach should say something along the lines of, "Get your right side behind the ball, not your body!" If you were to get your body behind the ball, your body would have to move laterally and contain an axis tilt. The body should pivot rotationally, not laterally.

4. *Resist the throw-out*

If you use the ground on the backswing and the arms have the same characteristics as the body, then gravity can access the club. When you push up on the ground, the club drops towards the impact zone. Remember, the arms are heavy and loose. What is heavy going up is light coming down. This prevents throw-out.

5. *Smaller moment of inertia creates bigger mass to hit with*

Because the arms are dead and have the body's characteristics on the takeaway, they stay on the same tilt as they started. This enables the club and its sweet spot to stay closer to the body's rotation, creating more depth in the golf swing and small moments of inertia. On the downswing with loft on the clubface and the shaft under the right shoulder, gravity can access the club, which resists throw-out and keeps the moment of inertia smaller. This enables the player to use more mass to hit the ball, and the body will stall less at impact as power is being released through the arms to the clubface to propel the ball.

This takes us on to COAM. The lower body swing harnesses one of the laws governing physical matter. This is called Conservation of Angular Momentum (COAM). Physics tells us that when an object rotates around a fixed axis, it rotates at a constant speed provided the object stays at the same distance from the axis. If the object is brought closer to the axis, it automatically speeds up. Likewise, if it is moved further away from the axis, it slows down. So a small moment of inertia adheres to the law of COAM.

c. Research

EMG research has demonstrated that the lower body swing uses different muscles than the conventional swing,[3] but we wanted to know how this swing produces clubhead speed.

1. *Purpose*

To determine how the lower body swing produces clubhead speed.

2. *Methods*

We used multi-mode, dynamic measurements, video recordings, force plates, an accelerometer, a goniometer and a radar swing speed device for 22 male golfers between the ages of 18 and 72.

---

3   *ASCM, 2014*

3. Results

Three variables were highly correlated to swing speed: vertical force on the ground under the left foot (scratch $r=0.80$, handicap $r=0.61$); total Newtons of force during the downswing (scratch $r=0.80$, handicap $r=0.61$); and vertical acceleration of the body (scratch $r=0.79$, handicap $r=0.75$). Other measured variables, including total degrees of knee flexion, knee flexing time and horizontal rotation were not highly correlated to swing speed.

Comparing the tracings of vertical force to the video demonstrated that the force began at the transition and continued past impact, which occurred soon after the initiation. This data means that the vertical force generates an inertial impulse, rather than being summed cumulatively. We verified this by having golfers use minimum knee flexion while still pushing down hard.

The accelerometer tracings show that vertical acceleration of the body from the inertial impulse is translated into horizontal acceleration (rotation) of the body. It also causes the body to accelerate onto the left leg.

The average left knee flexion of all golfers was 30 degrees to a final leg angle of 122 degrees.

4. Conclusions

The transverse pivot of the lower body swing generates an inertial impulse. The inertial impulse generates the sequence of body movements called the "kinetic chain," including rotation and movement onto the left side. These movements create clubhead speed on the downswing.

The optimum angle for left knee flexion is 120 degrees which, we discovered, is the same as in climbing stairs, jumping and other sports. We determined that scratch golfers make better use of ground forces than handicap golfers.

The lower body swing differs from the conventional swing in creating no torque between hips and shoulders. It requires no lateral axis tilt and no lifting of the club above the right shoulder. Therefore the lower body swing is protective of the lower back, shoulders, elbows and wrists.

As we age, our handicaps go up (we assigned 30 handicaps to beginners):

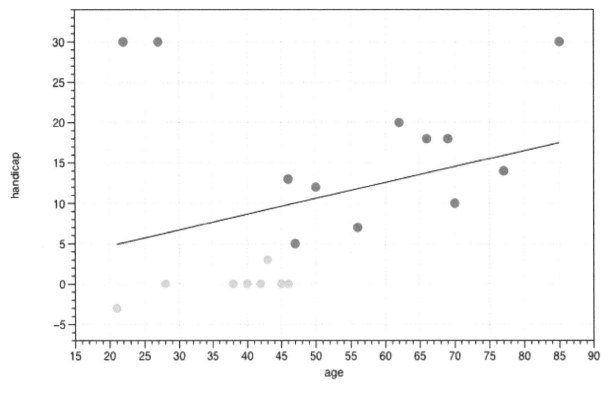

Graph 1

and our swing speeds go down:

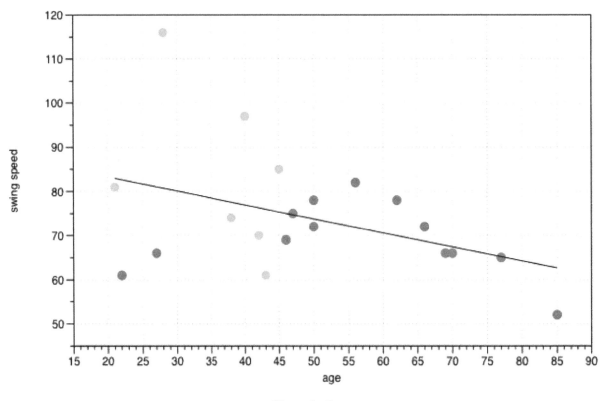

Graph 2

So it isn't surprising that the time it takes to flex and extend our left knee goes up:

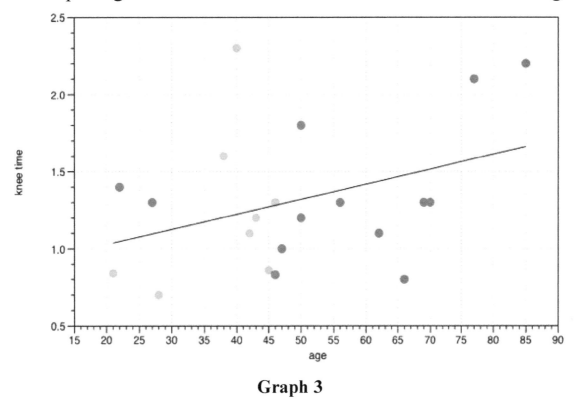

Graph 3

and the total force we produce under our left foot goes down.

Despite ageing, older golfers can flex the left knee just as much as younger golfers can:

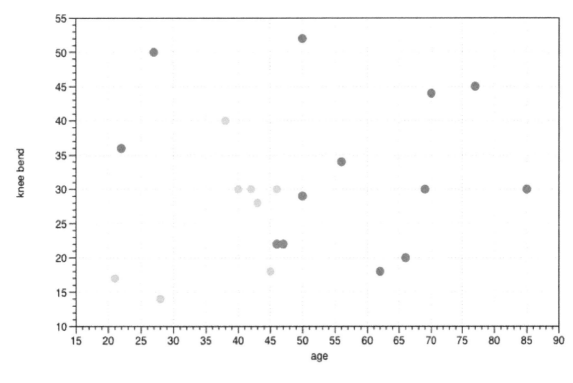

Graph 4

and as a consequence they can produce force over weight on one foot just as well as younger golfers:

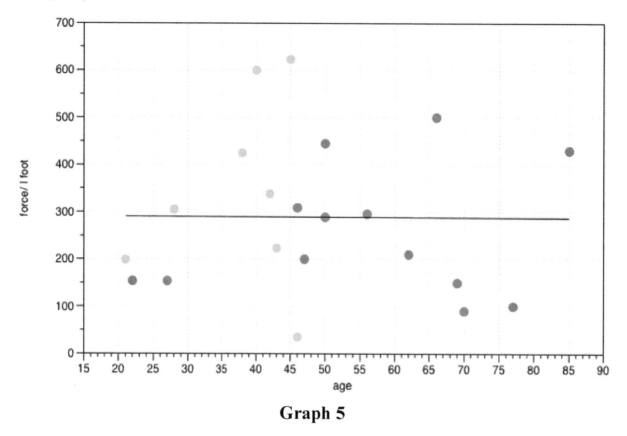

Graph 5

which means their vertical acceleration is even better than younger golfers:

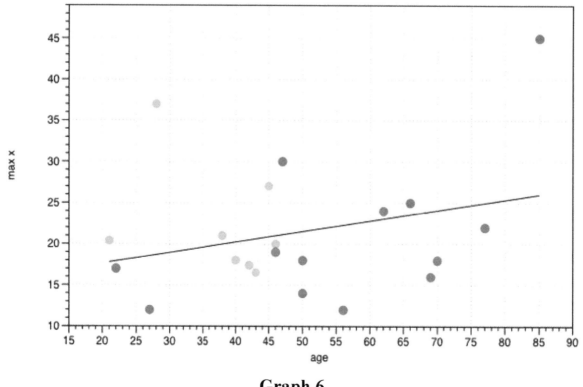

Graph 6

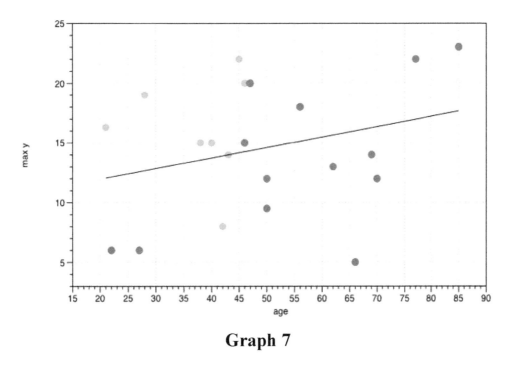

Graph 7

For the following set we asked the question, "Which variables we measured and calculated contribute most to swing speed?" We did this even though swing speed is probably only an approximate, and incomplete, measure of swing quality. But it is a measure we can use for our discussions while understanding that it is a limited criterion.

Many variables turn out to offer little correlation to swing speed. (In the following graphs, assume the steepness of the fit line to mean correlation significance.) For example, swing speed appears to slow down only slightly as knee time increases:

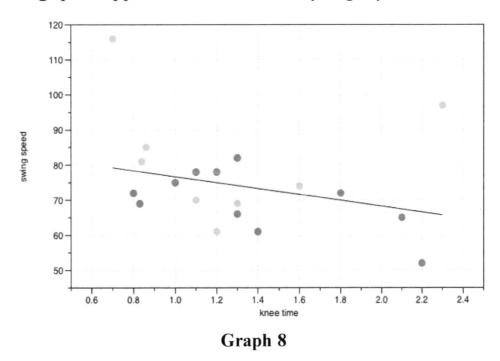

Graph 8

And the force produced by the left foot, minus body weight on one foot, also appears to only slightly increase swing speed:

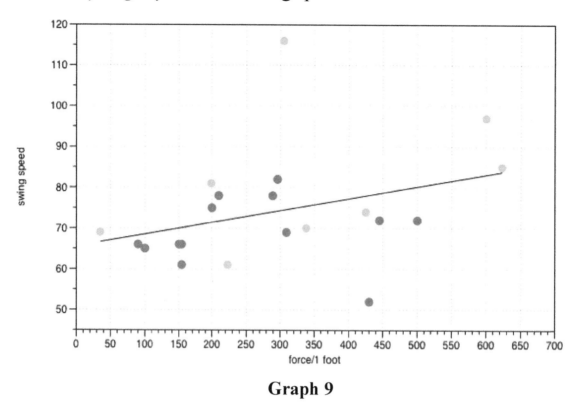

Graph 9

So we should not be surprised that vertical acceleration has a small effect on swing speed:

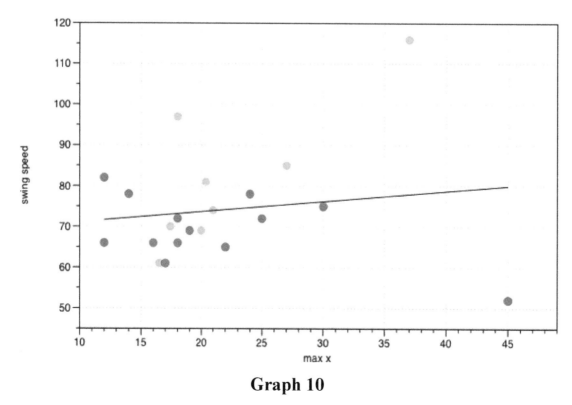

Graph 10

and that horizontal acceleration also has a small effect on swing speed:

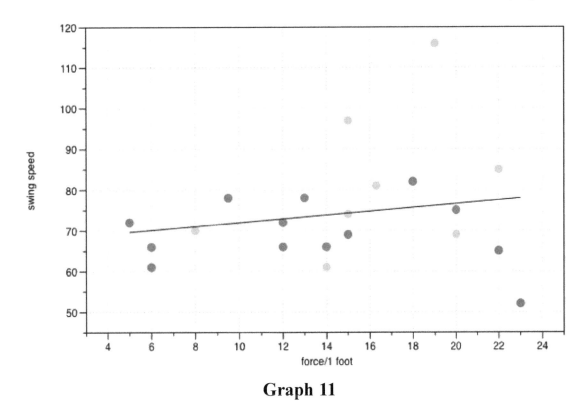

Graph 11

So does any parameter affect swing speed significantly? Yes, there are two – knee angle:

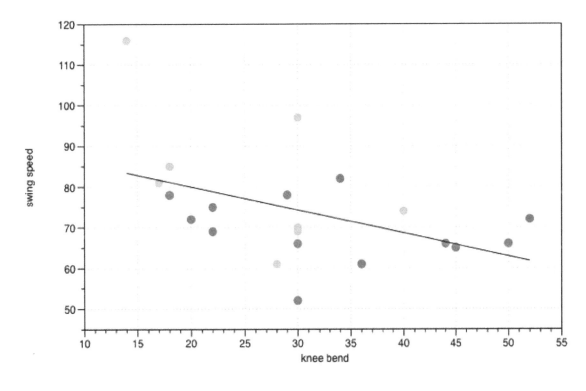

Graph 12

and total force under left foot:

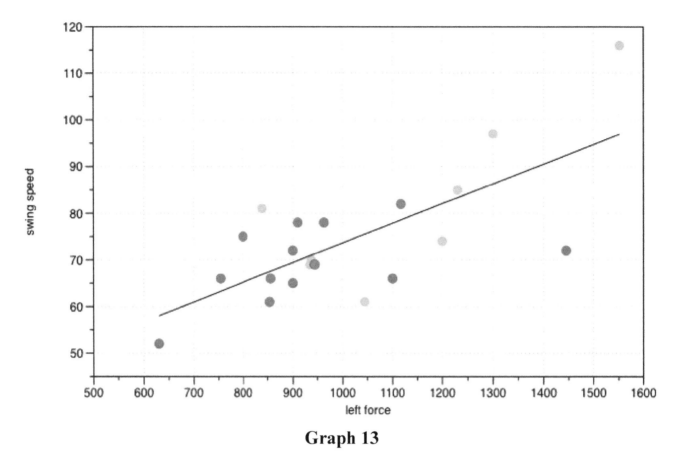

Graph 13

This requires some exploration. Graph 12 says that *less* knee flexion is correlated to more swing speed. This result could be understood as a skew in the data produced by a few subjects who have high swing speeds but small knee bends. Or it could be understood to say that the actual amount of knee bend is less important than something else (graph 13). We are impressed by the cluster of green dots around 30 degrees. This suggests that around 30 degrees is an optimum that better players find. Graph 12 strongly suggests that knee bends of greater and less than 30 degrees are sub-optimum.

However, graph 13 has an even steeper slope (rise/run) that says that the most important variable is total force produced. We interpret these two graphs together to be in support of the hypothesis that what matters most in generating swing speeds is the inertial impulse that is generated by an extending knee pushing on the ground.

It will take work on the range to find out what knee angle generates the greatest inertial impulse. Put simply, this analysis suggests that pushing harder is more important than flexing more.

Graph 14 suggests that the subject started with a flexed knee (130 degrees), extended it (to 160 degrees) and then rapidly flexed it (to 90 degrees) The little wobble on the way down in the bend is interesting because it exactly coincides with the peak in force. It may have to do with the club swinging by, and it may have to do with the foot rolling over.

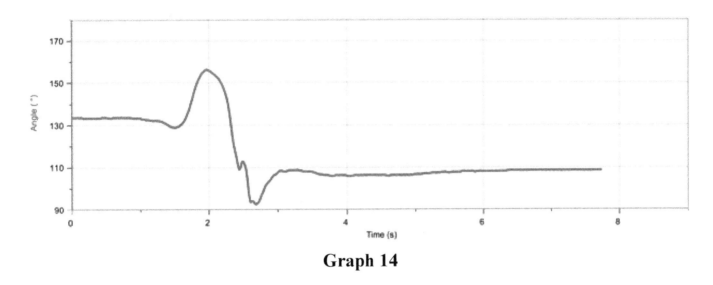

Graph 14

The effect on the force plate was an increase in force as the leg extended (before two seconds) then a return to baseline, then a rapid increase in force (after two seconds). We believe impact occurred exactly at the peak, after two seconds.

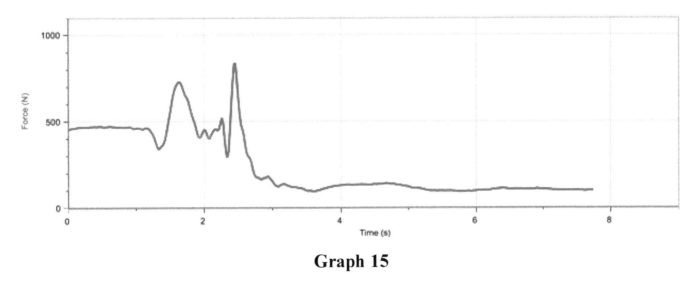

Graph 15

So this means two things: first the subject does not kink their knee at the top of the backswing. Second, and quite significantly, they create force with the right leg by flexing the knee.

Let us now look at the following force charts. If we add the left and right foot peak forces (939 + 634) we get 1570 newtons. Assuming the force were used to raise the body by one meter (probably too big) in 0.6 seconds (the time of the force generation), this gives a power of 2625 watts (3.5 horsepower).

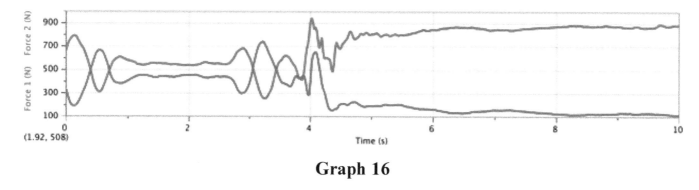

Graph 16

If we take someone who produces the same left foot force and no right force, as in graph 17, we have 934 newtons raising the body by the same one meter (again too big) in 0.6 seconds, which gives a power of 1556 watts (2.1 horsepower). This means that with the same effort, the second subject is only producing 0.6 of the power of the first subject. (It is possible that some of the right foot power that occurs when the second subject shifts their weight from right to left before impact increases their rotation.)

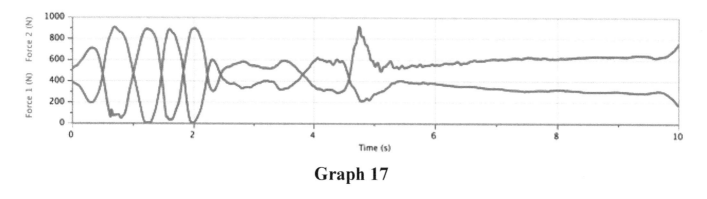

Graph 17

So the conclusion is to use both feet, and to do it quickly.

d. Unknowns that need to be investigated

The lower back is commonly susceptible to injury in the classic golf swing (upper body). During the swing, the hip joints and thoracic spine are limited in their movement so the lumbar spine sacrifices stability to obtain more movement. This irregular movement in the lumbar spine created by the axis tilt can be one of the main causes of injuries in the lower back. Limited spine and hip movement are two common findings in male golfers.

We believe that, owing to the absence of the axis tilt in the lower body swing, research is needed to show that there would be fewer injuries using this approach than in the classic swing and their rivals.

We believe our approach would be of interest to other parties carrying out research on the lower back.

Chapter 11

How the lower body swing differs from other approaches

a.   Conventional (upper body) swing

b.   Stack and tilt

c.   Others

Beginners, children and adults of all ages are being taught plane of the golf swing as their introduction to golf. This is like the times tables to math, and the dictionary to English – an absolute necessity. At the moment there are various approaches to teaching golf: the conventional classic swing, the stack and tilt, one plane and right-sided golf. But nothing is as simple and injury free as the lower body swing.

I hear you ask, "Why are you so confident that the lower body swing is understandable and reduces the risk of injury?"

We believe there are three main reasons:

- No axis tilt

- Transverse pivot

- Loft on the clubface.

All the other approaches mentioned have a lateral motion on the downswing. This axis tilt is a bending backwards with a bump of the hips towards the target. This motion puts strain on the lower back and can cause lower back injury. This movement is not present in the lower body swing.

The transverse body pivot eradicates any lateral motion in the golf swing. It is a front-to-back, back-to-front weight shift pushing against the ground to create pure rotation. Any swing, including an axis tilt, must contain a lateral shift.

Also, the other approaches conduct a square (open) and closed clubface at the terminus of the backswing. The lower body swing doesn't! We are just concerned that there is loft on the clubface. Loft is defined as a "backward slope, measured in degrees of the face of a golf club's head." The term "loft" means that the grooves of the clubface point towards the sky at the top of the backswing.

These three motions are unique to the lower body swing. It introduces a unique kinaesthetic feel consistently in sync with the laws of physics and mechanics. It is a question of mechanics over opinion.

Chapter 12

Injury prevention – to save your back

a. Backswing

b. Downswing

c. Impact

d. Finish

Responding to Sean Foley's upper body swing golf digest article

In 2010, Sean Foley offered four hints to help prevent lower back injury. These were:

- Backswing: to maintain a flexed right knee and to turn the left shoulder downwards.

- Downswing: to use the ground to create the swing. It feels as if the player is preparing to jump up using the thigh muscles and glutes in a squat move.

- Impact: 90% of the body weight should be over the left leg, and the shoulders and hips should be level and turning open.

- Finish: thrust the pelvis towards the target, absorbing the stress with the left glutes and core muscles. Push forward and stand up.[4]

---

4 Sean Foley, 'Four steps to save your back', Golf Digest, March 2010. Foley went on to work with Tiger Woods, Justin Rose and many more PGA tour players. He is regarded as one of the best golf coaches in the world. On this article he collaborated with Craig Davies, a chiropractor and fitness trainer.

a. Backswing

We believe that the transverse body pivot, front-to-back, back-to-front weight shift, will allow the right leg to extend without putting stress on the bottom vertebrae. This pivot makes behind the ball behind your head, not to the right of the ball. Any lateral movement to the right of the ball (the upper swing is behind the ball) will create a movement at the start of the downswing which will put torque on the spine. The proposed weight shift will not.

b. Downswing

The lateral squat on the downswing will be followed by an axis tilt which will put pressure on the spine. Our transverse pivot creates a movement down into the ground on the backswing and a push up off the ground on the downswing. This vertical force creates greater rotation than trying to rotate, which we have proved by way of scientific research. Our swing is without any lateral motion and therefore greatly reduces the risk of injury.

c. Impact

At impact, the lower body swing is not trying to rotate. The player is trying to push up from the ground for both feet. This vertical push will rotate the body. Once again, no lateral motion, and no ouch!

d. Finish

There is no thrusting forward of the pelvis towards the target. The lower body swing finishes the launch from the ground with a balanced finish, with no arch in the back, and the player's weight is over their left side. Once again there is no lateral motion or axis tilt, and no stress on the spine.

As mentioned earlier, Morowitz says, "The purpose of this book is to discuss and present evidence for the general thesis that the flow of energy through a system acts to organise a system."[5] We believe that we have discovered this in the lower body swing, and that the pushing against and off the ground recruits the right muscles to coordinate the body's flow of energy to drive the golf swing without injury.

---

5   Morowitz, *Energy Flow in Biology.*

Lightning Source UK Ltd.
Milton Keynes UK
UKHW050127130819
347832UK00003B/31/P